SPOTTING DIFFERENCES

Cheetah
or
Leopard?

by Kirsten Chang

BELLWETHER MEDIA • MINNEAPOLIS, MN

Note to Librarians, Teachers, and Parents:

Blastoff! Readers are carefully developed by literacy experts and combine standards-based content with developmentally appropriate text.

Level 1 provides the most support through repetition of high-frequency words, light text, predictable sentence patterns, and strong visual support.

Level 2 offers early readers a bit more challenge through varied simple sentences, increased text load, and less repetition of high-frequency words.

Level 3 advances early-fluent readers toward fluency through increased text and concept load, less reliance on visuals, longer sentences, and more literary language.

Level 4 builds reading stamina by providing more text per page, increased use of punctuation, greater variation in sentence patterns, and increasingly challenging vocabulary.

Level 5 encourages children to move from "learning to read" to "reading to learn" by providing even more text, varied writing styles, and less familiar topics.

Whichever book is right for your reader, Blastoff! Readers are the perfect books to build confidence and encourage a love of reading that will last a lifetime!

This edition first published in 2020 by Bellwether Media, Inc.

No part of this publication may be reproduced in whole or in part without written permission of the publisher. For information regarding permission, write to Bellwether Media, Inc., Attention: Permissions Department, 6012 Blue Circle Drive, Minnetonka, MN 55343.

Library of Congress Cataloging-in-Publication Data

Names: Chang, Kirsten, 1991- author.
Title: Cheetah or Leopard? / by Kirsten Chang.
Description: Minneapolis, MN : Bellwether Media, Inc., [2020] | Series: Blastoff! Readers: Spotting Differences |
    Audience: Age 5-8. | Audience: K to Grade 3. | Includes bibliographical references and index.
Identifiers: LCCN 2018054609 (print) | LCCN 2018056489 (ebook) |
    ISBN 9781618915740 (ebook) | ISBN 9781644870334 (hardcover : alk. paper)
Subjects: LCSH: Cheetah--Juvenile literature. | Leopard--Juvenile literature.
Classification: LCC QL737.C23 (ebook) | LCC QL737.C23 C445 2020 (print) | DDC 599.75/9--dc23
LC record available at https://lccn.loc.gov/2018054609

Editor: Al Albertson   Designer: Jeffrey Kollock

Printed in the United States of America, North Mankato, MN.

Table of Contents

Cheetahs and Leopards

Cheetahs and leopards are both big cats. They are **mammals** with spotted fur.

leopard

Both cats live in the grasslands. They hunt other animals. How can you tell them apart?

cheetahs

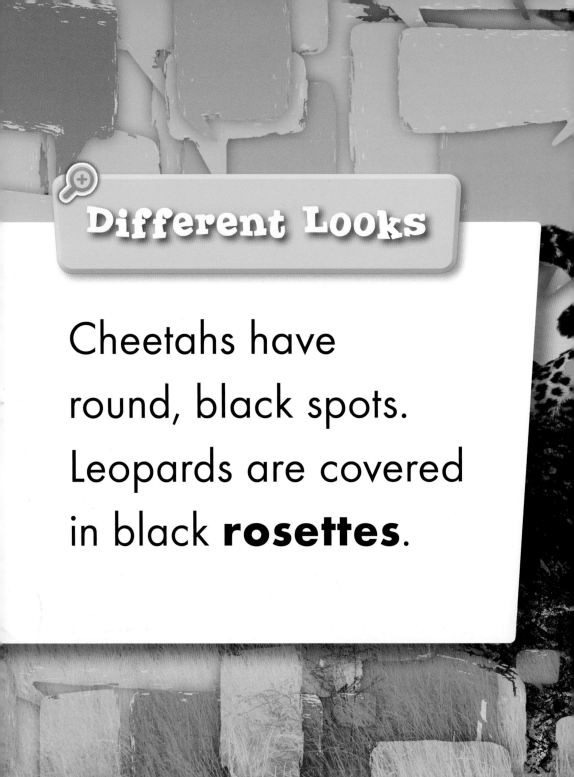

Cheetahs have round, black spots. Leopards are covered in black **rosettes**.

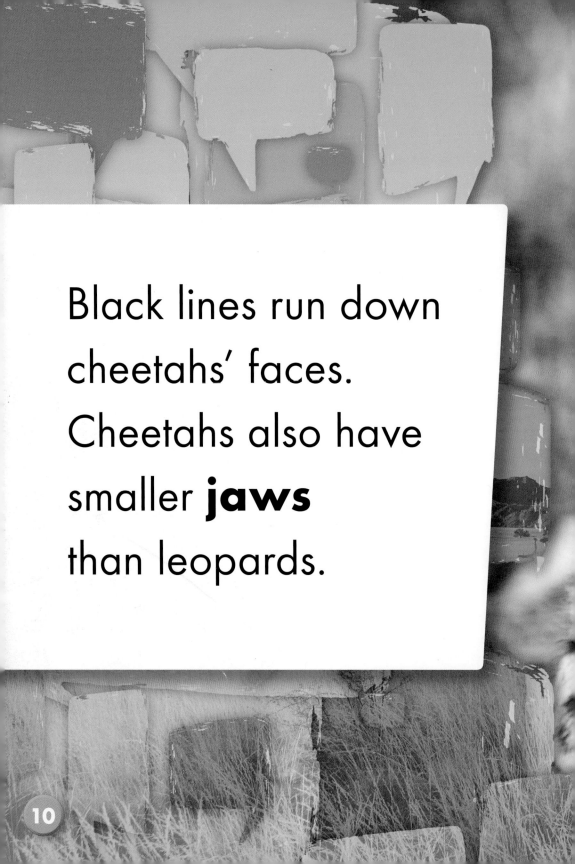

Black lines run down cheetahs' faces. Cheetahs also have smaller **jaws** than leopards.

black
line →

jaw →

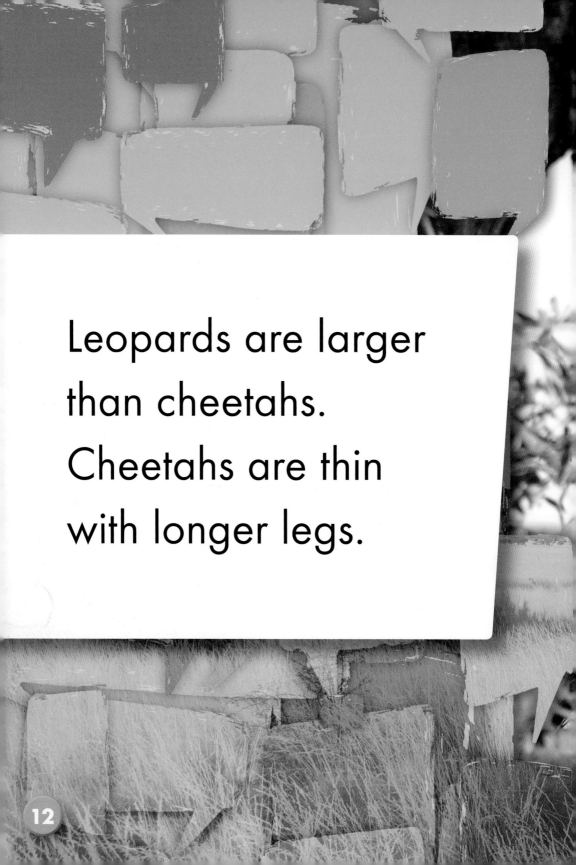

Leopards are larger than cheetahs. Cheetahs are thin with longer legs.

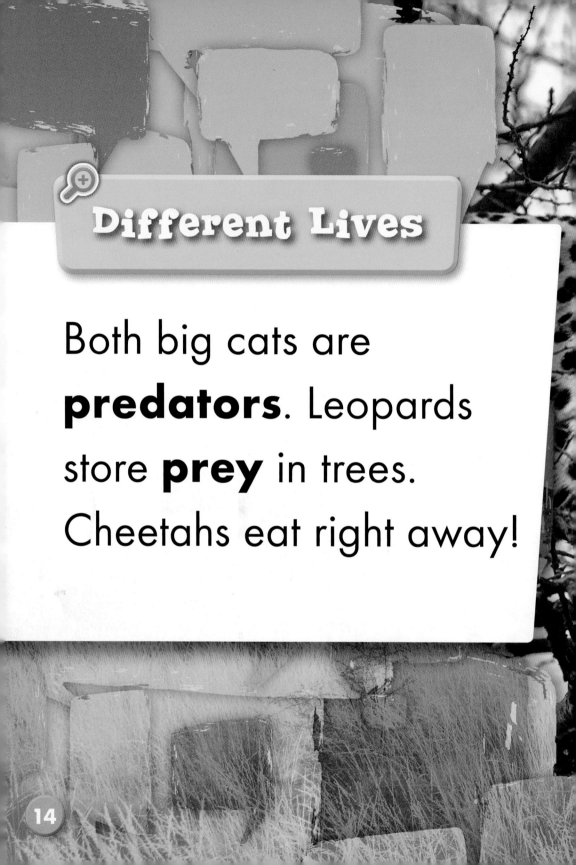

Both big cats are **predators**. Leopards store **prey** in trees. Cheetahs eat right away!

prey

Cheetahs hunt
during the day.
Leopards hunt at night.

Cheetahs run fast
to catch prey.
Leopards hide
and surprise prey.
Which big cat is this?

Side by Side

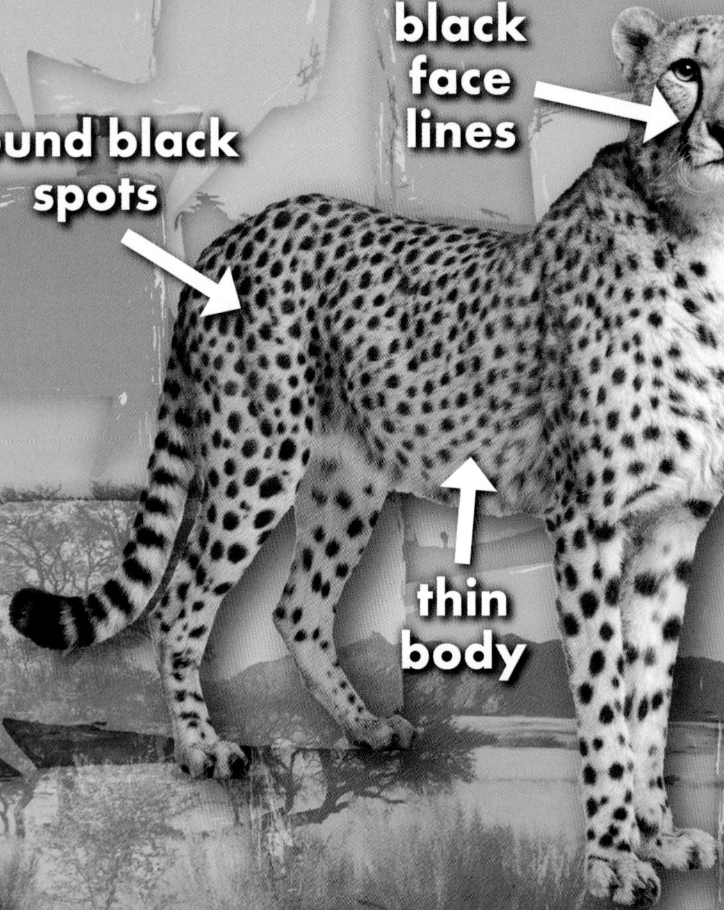

black
face
lines

round black
spots

small
jaw

thin
body

Cheetah Differences

hunt during
the day

use speed
to hunt

eat prey
right away

black rosettes

large
jaw

thicker body

Leopard Differences

hunt at night

use strength to hunt

hide prey in trees

Glossary

jaws

the lower part of an animal's mouth

prey

animals hunted by other animals for food

mammals

warm-blooded animals that have hair and feed their young milk

rosettes

spots in the shape of roses

predators

animals that hunt other animals for food

To Learn More

AT THE LIBRARY

Archer, Claire. *Leopards*. Minneapolis, Minn.: Abdo Kids, 2015.

Herrington, Lisa M. *Cheetahs and Leopards*. New York, N.Y.: Children's Press, 2016.

Statts, Leo. *Cheetahs*. Minneapolis, Minn.: Abdo Zoom, 2017.

ON THE WEB

FACTSURFER

Factsurfer.com gives you a safe, fun way to find more information.

1. Go to www.factsurfer.com.

2. Enter "cheetah or leopard" into the search box and click 🔍.

3. Select your book cover to see a list of related web sites.

Index

The images in this book are reproduced through the courtesy of: JMx Images, front cover (cheetah);
Alex van Schaik, front cover (leopard), pp. 4-5; Vaganundo_Che, pp. 6-7; GUDKOV ANDREY, pp. 8-9;
Suzanne Marie Richcreek, pp. 9, 22 (rosettes); Kevin Standage, pp. 10-11; Pedro Helder Pinheiro, p. 11 (jaw);
Maggy Meyer, pp. 12-13; Anton_Ivanov, p. 13 (bubble); Sourabh Bharti, p. 17 (bubble); Shahin Olakara,
pp. 18-19; Eric Isselee, p. 20 (cheetah); Gary C. Tognoni, p. 20 (daytime); Elana Erasmus, p. 20 (speed);
Sergey Novikov, p. 20 (eat right away); Eric Isselee, p. 21 (leopard); Albie Venter, p. 21 (night); mario.bono,
p. 21 (strength); Ewan Chesser, p. 21 (hide prey); Sue Green, p. 22 (jaws); GUDKOV ANDREY, p. 22 (mammals);
Mike V. Shuman, p. 22 (predators); Gary C Tognoni, p. 22 (prey).